David Scott

Outside the Box

An interior designer's innovative approach to creating chic and comfortable rooms

Principal photography: Antoine Bootz

Editorial director: Suzanne Slesin
Design: Stafford Cliff
Managing editor: Regan Toews
Production: Dominick J. Santise, Jr.
Assistant editor: Deanna Kawitzky
Interviews: Barbara Dixon

POINTED LEAF PRESS, LLC.
WWW.POINTEDLEAFPRESS.COM

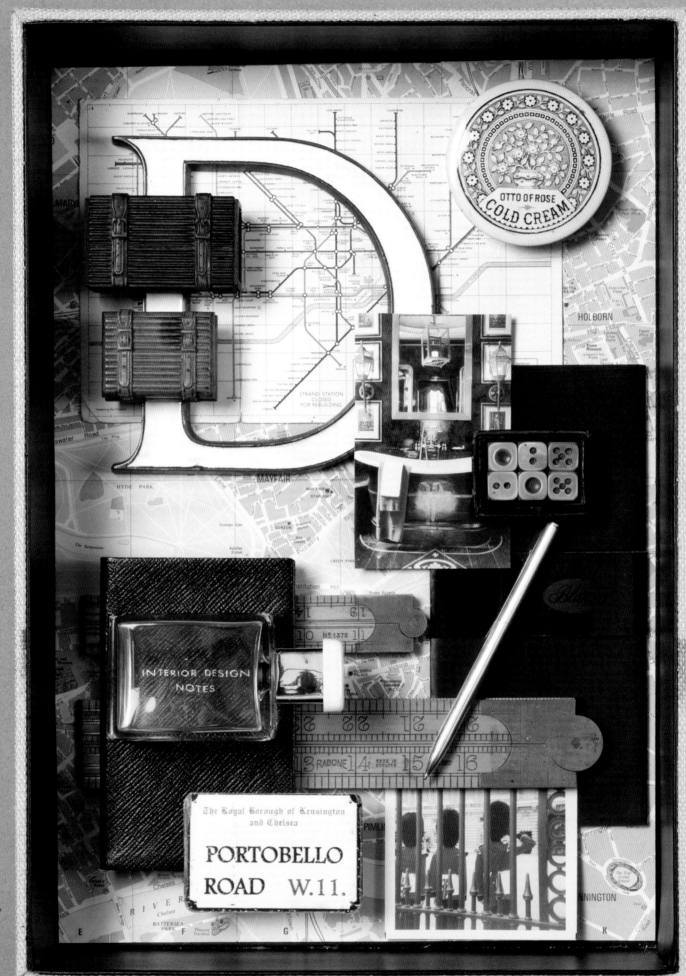

LONDON
A ceramic box, a bit of British history and one of David's many finds at the flea market along Portobello Road, discovering Blake's hotel, and a snapshot of the guards at Buckingham Palace are some of David's inspirational memories from London.

An intuitive designer with a flair for color and texture, space, and proportion

David Scott's work ethic as an interior designer, and his attitude toward his clients, is unusual if not unique in a profession where striking the right balance between ego and service is often precarious. Nevertheless, for David, getting to know his clients, including how they have lived and how they may want to live, is at the core of his practice. "I'm interested in creating what I call 'client-centric' homes," he explained. "I look at the practical, functional side of their lives, while also respecting the architecture and the surrounding environment." That can include observing the way daylight enters an apartment or house, and how it changes throughout the day, as well as the climate particular to a location, whether it be by the water or in the desert, in the city or in the countryside. Are there views to be considered? What can be done to make such mundane things as air conditioning and heating ducts more glamorous and even decorative? "Color," he said, "defines how you feel when you are in a room." But eliciting or defining that sensibility, that preference, that reaction from a client is sometimes the most challenging part of a project: "My job is to distill all these things and make sure certain threads come through. My goal is to end up with rooms that progress and flow naturally." David's own career path began in Westchester, New York, where he was raised in the 1960s in a "California Contemporary" suburban house filled with Danish Modern furniture. "A family from Shanghai lived up the street," he recalled, "and their house was done with furniture by Charles Eames and Mies van der Rohe, and had a more hard-edged and contemporary look than I had seen before." Although the look of the interior was different, David came to the conclusion that no matter the style people chose to live with, their basic needs were the same. David was also influenced by being exposed to his parents' friends, many of whom were in the arts, a grandmother who took pride in her fine furniture and objects, and his aunt, Karen, who allowed him, very early on, to use her house as a laboratory for his emerging decorating talents. By many accounts, David was also a very inquisitive child. "My mother would tell me that even when I was very young, I would always ask where everything came from, what it cost, and how it was made," he said. "Part of being a designer and artist is about curiosity and being like a sponge," he added, "looking at things and seeing something different each time." After a liberal arts education in college, David worked in the hotel business. "That's where I learned to anticipate people's needs," he said. At the Pierre, one of New York's top luxury hotels, he learned about pampering clients and making sure they received whatever they wanted. "It's called service," he added.

"And interior design is first and foremost a service business." Eventually, David went back to school at the New York School of Interior Design, got another Bachelor of Arts, and started his own interior design business while he was still a student. In the beginning, he worked out of his home, and then, in 1993, opened an office on 57th Street in Manhattan. From the time he took his first trip to England as a 15 year old, David has observed, absorbed, and eventually translated his discoveries and reactions into his interior design schemes. In London, David lived with a family and traveled with a group all over the country. It was 1976. He photographed the Queen's Guard outside Buckingham Palace, and his long attraction to what he sees in London, "a city of contrasts," began. He admires the English love of manners, the proper way of doing things, the pride that they take in what they do. He started collecting old jars and containers—"bits of history," he said. These would translate later into the "smalls" that made their way into his different homes and onto his clients' coffee tables. Objects like vintage rulers and wood-turned urns would appeal to him because of their patina and as pieces of functional art. Years later, going back to London on his own or with clients, he discovered Blake's Hotel and its dramatic eclectic décor, with its strong use of black. "It was so daring," he recalled, "I was buzzing with excitement when I first went there. Not that I do black rooms, but there was a gutsiness about the whole place that I never forgot." Paris, which he first visited when he was in his mid-twenties, bowled him over with its symmetry and deliberateness. "My sense of architecture was heightened," David recalled. "In Paris, standards are extremely high." Walking all over, David loved the parks—especially the Jardin du Luxembourg and the Tuileries—with their allées of majestic trees. Then there was Hermès. "A mecca!" he declared. "The shop always has new things. I love their impeccable craftsmanship, their classicism, their attention to detail." The Picasso Museum in the Marais was also a favorite—a centuries-old building re-interpreted with plaster light fixtures and white walls. On to Italy and the island of Capri, where David fell under the spell of a lifestyle that captured the essence of summer living. "Lemon trees, bougainvillea, and delicious food—nothing pretentious, even though it's pretty fancy," he said. Long days at the beach, relaxing and looking at the rocks in the sea along the coast, staying at La Scalinatella Hotel Capri—"a warm place that makes you feel cool, with its sense of hospitality, natural linens, and beautiful textures," said David—all became imprinted on David's way of seeing and enjoying the world.

PARIS
Grand boulevards, allées of trees, a love of architectural symmetry, the Picasso Museum, and the classic masculinity of Hermès designs continue to make Paris one of David's favorite cities.

CAPRI

The fragrance of lemon trees, the vibrant color of bougainvillea, and La Scalinatella Hotel Capri, with its warm welcome and natural linens, contribute to the relaxed atmosphere David loves on the Italian isle of Capri.

A designer who is sensitive to and delighted by the organic shapes in the natural world

David Scott is inspired by drops of water on a leaf. He is also thinking about the capillary action that allows the liquid to maintain its rounded form. Nature is full of magic tricks, and David, fascinated by the process, wants to penetrate the mysteries. For a moment, his thoughts dart to the reflections he is seeing in a collection of blown glass bubbles as they magnify and distort the space they inhabit. Then David returns to contemplating water. This time his curiosity is expressed in delight as he ponders the divining-rod essence of the branching patterns created by rivers and streams. He remarks on the intensity of transformation as the convergence becomes a delta on Mother Earth, opening to the sea. The conversation skips now, moving upward to stormy skies on the verge of purging, and the unique textures of riverbeds.

Sedimentary rocks are not the only source of wonder and query for David. Growing up in Westchester exposed him to the dichotomy of hard—New York State schist outcroppings—covered with soft velvet carpets of bright green moss. This and more he discovered in his own back yard. David often speaks of the tension between the order and disorder in nature he experienced in his formative years, exuding palpable delight that the joys of youthful discovery can be translated into one's life's work.

For me, collaborating with David was truly an organic experience. After architect Alexander Gorlin introduced us, to combine our energies and talents, we quickly found out that we shared a similar vocabulary and an enthusiasm for natural forms. I sometimes refer to this convergence as "worshipping at the same altar." The assortment of roots, sticks, seeds, and other flotsam and jetsam belonging to an urban hunter and gatherer found in the Doner Studio stimulated David's active imagination. Soon a length of exquisitely tangled roots, translated first in our mind's eye, later into cast bronze, became a monumental front door pull for a contemporary beach house. Then we assessed the large sheets of wax that lay propped against the walls of the studio, each worked by hand and heated into various patterns—representing growth, vines, coral formations, and beehives. After some consideration, and a visit to the construction site to ascertain scale and proportion, the waxes morphed into a frieze that moved throughout the living space, replacing traditional vents with panels that disguised the heating and air conditioning systems: with their white gold leaf finish, they brought beauty to the functional, and displaced any thought of the usual or mundane. David's clients were dazzled. So was I.

I enjoy David's extraordinary palettes of texture and tone. His arrangements for presentations are the works of an artist—Modernist still lifes that can stand on their own merit. All of this refinement and understanding blends with David's respect for the lives of others. The rooms he creates are picture perfect, yet livable. They are inviting. They beckon us to sit on one of his exceptional carpets as well as on a chair or couch, to fill a beautiful vase on the credenza with flowers, a leaf or a fern, to check out the dimmer on the light switch until you are in the zone of comfort you desire. As I reflect on the scope of David's work in interior design, I realize that he offers up a vision of living that has been distilled through the lens of time. It is no coincidence that his early work is steeped in classical reference. Using that period of intense interest as structure, David now refracts the vision through the prism of experience. This sheds a lot of light on the lives of those fortunate enough to be living in a space transformed by David's wand into the creation of their personal Eden.—MICHELE OKA DONER, October 2011

OPPOSITE In 2009, David created a striking and atmospheric room for a show house in New York that benefited the Breast Cancer Research Foundation, with artist Michele Oka Doner as his muse. Objects by the sculptor were displayed on the mid-1950s mother-of-pearl and brass table by Cesare Lacca, from Van den Akker in New York, and the French 1930s Art Deco console by René Prou, from Guy Regal Antiques Ltd. in New York. The lamp is a 1970s design by French designer Willy Daro and came from Todd Merrill Antiques in New York. The carpet is from Carini Lang.

FOLLOWING PAGES Images from the natural world—the surface of water, the texture of tree bark, a pattern in the sand, the color of ferns—inspire David in his work as a designer. These elements have been appropriated and transformed, resurfacing in the details of his own New York apartment, such as in the top of a table, the design of a rug, the texture of a sculpture, the translucence of glass, or the entrancing color combinations in a contemporary work of art.

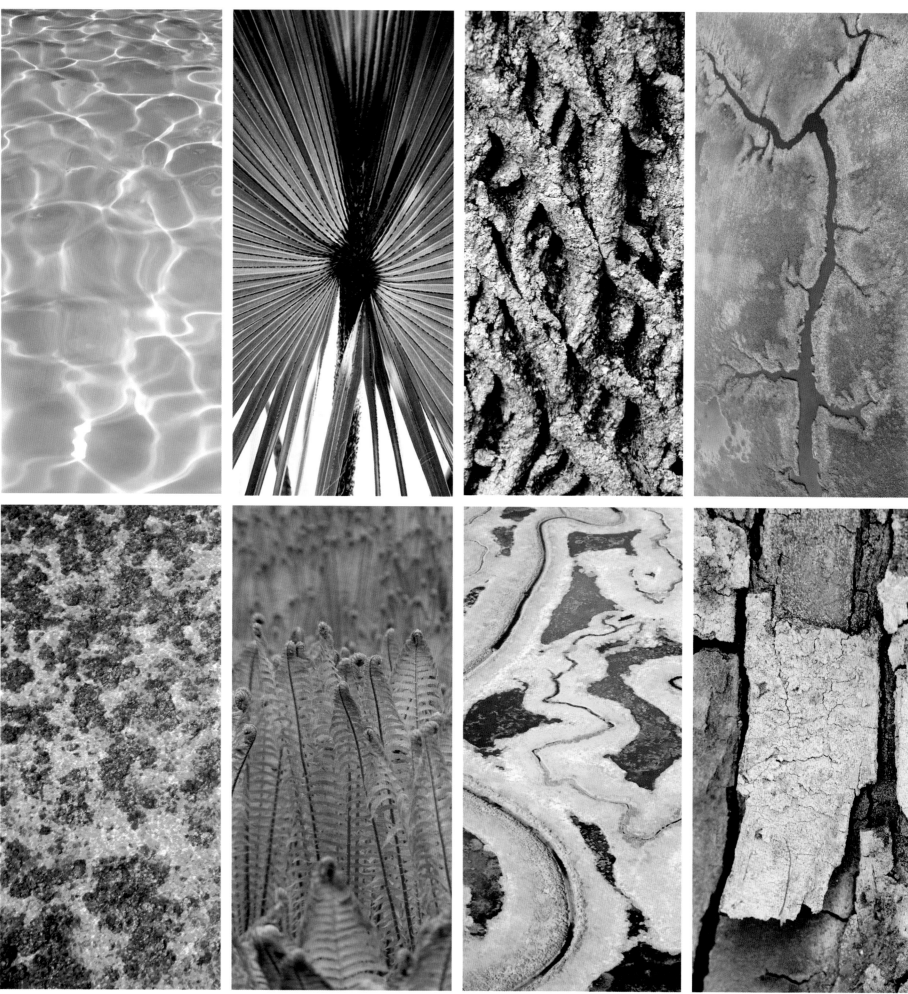

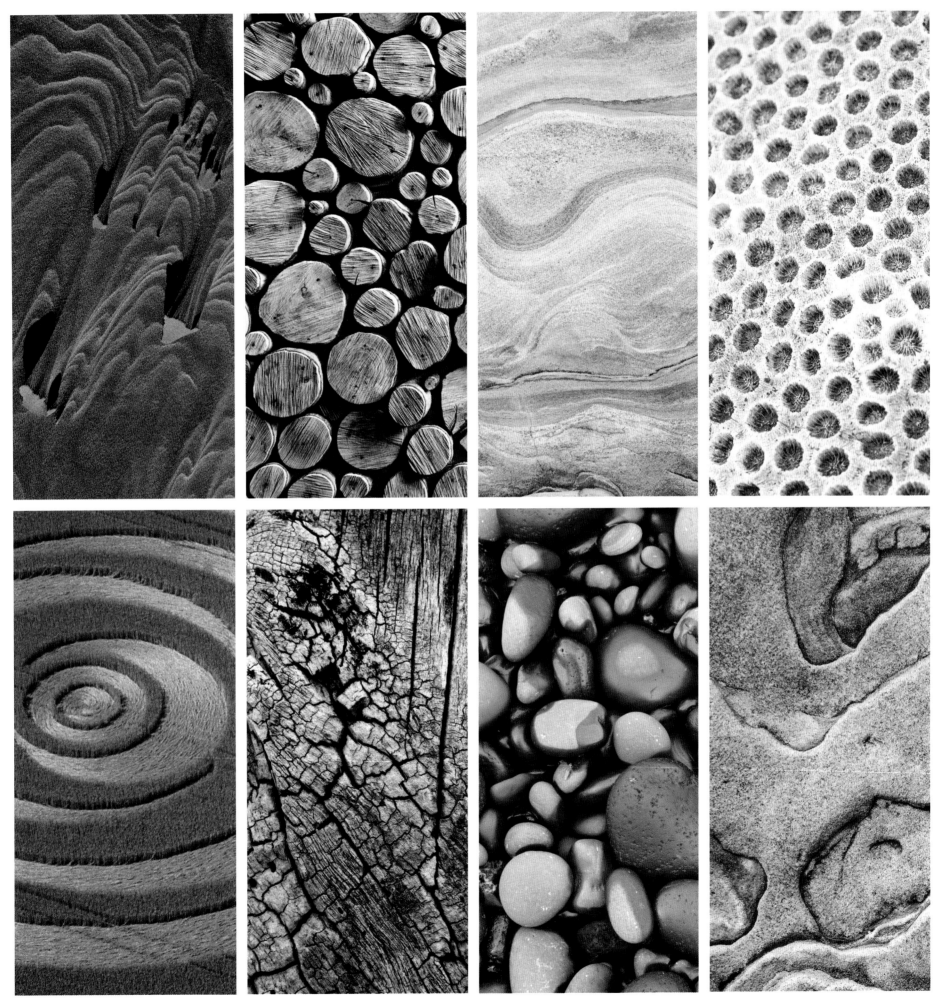

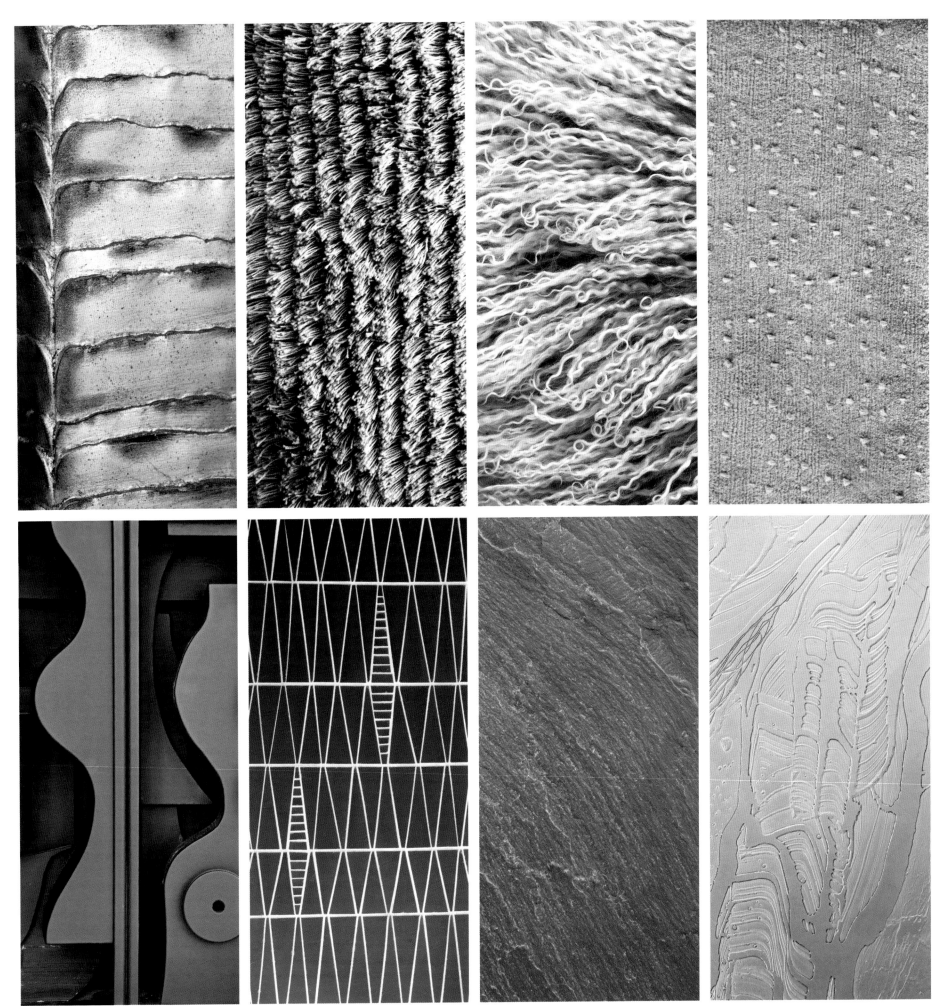

A contemporary urban apartment is given an edge of warmth and sensuality to create a comfortable, sophisticated home

Whenever we present an interior scheme to clients, we create mood boxes—compositions of materials and textures. But the feeling of a space does not come only from fabrics, wallpapers, and rugs. Sometimes the quality of light, the shape of the room, or the choice of furniture and art are just as important. That's why we include samples or photographs of these elements to give an overall impression. In the case of my Manhattan apartment, I have worked backwards to render the finished design into a demonstration of our technique. I introduced soft materials with minimalistic hardware to offset the strong architecture of both the exterior views and the interior spaces.

I knew I wanted to live in the United Nations Plaza in Manhattan when I first walked into the apartment, with its grand floor-to-ceiling windows, and felt its glamorous 1960s vibe. The co-op on the 15th floor was in perfect, vintage condition, and I knew I could make it fabulous. The building, designed by the firm Harrison Abramovitz & Harris in 1966, with its wonderful lobby and understated style, had such a strong grid. I was determined to respect the effortless style of the period, yet bring it up to date. In the apartment, I opened up the public spaces into an enfilade, and transformed the second bedroom into a library. Throughout the apartment, I unified the space with white plaster walls and floors of ebonized, cerused oak. Although I usually integrate an aspect of traditional design into my interiors, here I wanted to embrace the modern—even though I tend not to like the coolness often associated with it. I chose the shapes, forms, and warm color palette of the furnishings to soften the spaces and to contrast with the masculine severity of the architecture. The fluid lines of chairs by T.H. Robsjohn-Gibbings, Saporiti, and Thonet, for example, are sensual and elegant. Each of the pieces of furniture is beautiful and comfortable, appropriate, but not expected. As always, comfort is crucial. I am particularly drawn to the use of wood, especially in dark or caramel tones, because of its strength and warmth. I found just the right balance in my apartment by carefully editing and layering. My home, born first as a mid-1960s glass envelope, now embodies my twenty-first-century soul.

OPPOSITE The view from David's living room offers an ever-changing play of light on the grid of windows in the 1966 twin apartment building.

RIGHT In the entrance foyer, a 1940s X-frame iron and leather stool by French designer Jean-Michel Frank sits under two 2002 paintings by John Spinks, a British artist he discovered at a Miami Art Basel exhibition.

OVERLEAF A bookcase made from components by the Italian architect Antonio Citterio holds books, mementos, and objects that David has collected over the past 25 years.

Entertaining STEWART

GENTLEMAN

THE FINEST ROOMS in America

HEALTH CLUBS

IN THE ARTS & CRAFTS STYLE   Mayer/Gray   Chronicle Books

Christian Dior

RIVIERA COCKTAIL   Edward Quinn

MICHELE OKA DONER HUMANNATURE

ERIC FONTENEAU

HIP HOTELS   CITY

MAKING MARKS

ART DECO   COLEÇÃO BERARDO

DWELLINGS

Legendary Decorators of the Twentieth Century   Mark Hampton

ROOMS

SCULPTURE TODAY

Janette Laverrière

NEW YORK EXPOSED

PREVIOUS PAGES Ethan, to the left of Josie, David's longhaired dachshunds, are right at home in the designer's spacious and light-filled living room. A pair of 1970s suede-covered Italian chairs by Sergio and Giorgio Saporiti are next to a sofa by Christian Liaigre. The vintage credenza, which anchors one side of the room, is by Paul McCobb and comes from Homenature, a shop in Southampton, New York.

LEFT The English Regency table, from Niall Smith Antiques in New York, is one of the few pieces David brought from his former apartment. Behind it hangs *Harriet's Birthday*, a 1987 collage by Esteban Vicente, which came from the Ameringer McEnery Yohe Gallery in New York.

OPPOSITE The 1935 carved stone head of a woman, signed by German sculptor Johann Philip Lembke, was once in the collection of Roger Prigent, a well-known New York antiques dealer.

OPPOSITE *Serendipity*, a contemporary oil and gouache by James Kennedy, is part of a vignette that includes a small mobile by jewelry designer Robert Lee Morris, a shallow Lucite dish from Maison 24, a shop in New York, and *Night Blossom*, a 1973 work by American sculptor Louise Nevelson.

RIGHT Citterio designed the armchair covered in Mongolian lamb, which came from B&B Italia. A sculpture by American artist Frank Flynn, which David found at Lost City Arts in New York, stands by an ottoman by Robsjohn-Gibbings, the English designer.

OVERLEAF A 2008 photograph entitled *Bronzino: Ugolino Martelli*, by the German artist Reinhard Görner from Lumas, in New York, sets the scene in the atmospheric library. The sofa is upholstered in an Ultrasuede from Holly Hunt; the appliquéd and embroidered pillow is from Holland & Sherry; the pair of brass Modernist floor lamps came from Lorin Marsh; and the coffee table, a sculpted walnut- and slate-topped design, is by Phillip Lloyd Powell, a 1960s artist who worked in New Hope, Pennsylvania.

OPPOSITE AND RIGHT
A detail of a large 1982
work on paper entitled
Imola Three II, by
American artist Frank
Stella, is part of the
monochromatic color
scheme in the master
bedroom. A 1960s
lacquer side chair by
Gio Ponti, the Italian
architect, from Galerie
Van den Akker in New
York, is paired with a
mid-twentieth century
Robsjohn-Gibbings desk
from R.E. Steele Antiques
in East Hampton, New
York. The pastel is by the
early twentieth century
artist, Pavel Tchelitchew.

LEFT A Spode bowl and Wedgewood candlesticks are accessories that David collected years ago on one of his trips to Europe.

OPPOSITE Tall windows allow the maximum daylight into the dining area that has been furnished with a vintage 1970s burlwood Parsons table by Milo Baughman, the Modernist American designer. David surrounded it with his favorite Anziano chairs from Donghia.

OPPOSITE AND RIGHT The galley kitchen has been outfitted with cabinetry by Boffi. Chairs by Paul McCobb, from C.J. Peters in New York, are pulled up to a chrome-based, marble-topped table from Jonathan Adler. The Swedish alabaster chandelier, from Eileen Lane Antiques in New York, came from David's first Manhattan apartment.

A sense of drama enlivens a new Connecticut colonial house by giving it the feeling of a glamorous Manhattan townhouse

My clients knew they wanted to furnish their home with pieces that told a story and were distinctive. Through a combination of their interests and my knowledge, their sense of connoisseurship developed along with their passion for the decorative arts. The luxurious silk rugs, as well as many of the upholstered pieces of furniture, were designed especially for the house. The luxurious wall coverings and the unusual ceiling treatments convey the 'wow factor' that my clients desired. When all of these elements are carefully layered together, they create a truly dramatic effect.

My favorite clients are the ones that engage me in everything from the very beginning. I do my best work when I can be involved with the entirety of the project. This was the case when a couple—he is a builder and developer, and she is in the fashion business—and their two daughters decided to leave Manhattan and move to a newly built 10,000-square-foot Georgian Colonial house in Greenwich, Connecticut. Both of the clients have strong personalities and wanted the feeling of a glamorous New York townhouse, but were not sure how this would translate in the suburbs. As much as it was a learning process for them, it was invigorating and wonderful to work with such energetic people, who were thrilled about the process. It made the collaboration that much more rewarding. Even though they didn't know what they wanted specifically, they were willing to take risks and were interested in making strong statements. They wanted the interiors to be sensational and trusted me implicitly—understanding the costs involved, what was available in the marketplace, and the craftsmanship of the pieces I was showing them. We were on an exciting journey together.

PREVIOUS PAGES The Greenwich, Connecticut, house, with its fieldstone exterior and chimneys, was newly built in the Georgian Colonial style, which fit in well with the historic estates in the area.

RIGHT The front door opens onto a grand double ceiling-height entrance foyer. To balance the formality of the space, David chose Sisal, a grasscloth wall covering from Stark Fabric in a rich Prussian blue, contrasting it with the crisp white-painted door frames, wainscoting, and moldings. The designer commissioned Carolina Sardi, a Miami, Florida–based Argentinean artist, to create the enameled steel installation that hangs over the fireplace.

LEFT In the entrance foyer, a round, custom-made silk carpet by Carini Lang echoes the grain of the antique cherry tabletop of an early nineteenth-century Biedermeier center table from Ritter Antik in New York.

OPPOSITE A bench by Dallas-based interior designer Jan Showers, upholstered in a Kravet fabric, stands under a French 1950s shield-shaped sconce with black églomisé glass that is one of a pair. The Maison Jansen sconces came from Flair Home, a shop in New York, and recall the shape of the leaded glass windows.

RIGHT One side of the living room was furnished with a large custom-made sofa in the Maison Jansen-style from F. Schumacher & Co. The pillows are upholstered in luxurious velvet fabrics from Lee Jofa and Rose Tarlow. The side chair is from Mecox Gardens and has been upholstered in chenille from Jim Thompson. "The unusual red chair is an exciting punctuation point in the room," said David. The abstract painting above the sofa, *Breaking Dawn*, is a 1996 acrylic on canvas by Ronnie Landfield, an American artist.

OVERLEAF LEFT In the living room, gilded ceramic accessories sit on a 2005 round side table by Piero Fornasetti from Galerie Van den Akker.

OVERLEAF RIGHT A 1970s metal starburst by C. Jeré, from Flair Home, has been placed on a brass-legged table with an agate top, which was designed by David Scott Interiors. The colors of the stone coordinate with the pattern of the rug.

PREVIOUS PAGES David decided to choose a series of sensuous curved shapes to offset the classic straight lines of the living room fireplace. A pair of 1950s armchairs by the Italian designer Marco Zanuso, covered in a chocolate brown velvet, which came from Bernd Goeckler Antiques in New York, have been placed across from a curved, tufted sofa upholstered in a velvet from Romo. *The Muse*, a 2008 mixed-media painting by James Kennedy, a young contemporary artist, hangs above the fireplace. A Murano glass knot and a gilded bronze leaf dish, both from Mecox Gardens, and an amber glass vase, from H.B. Home in East Hampton, New York, are arranged on an oval 1940s Hungarian Art Deco cocktail table from Szalon Antiques in Los Angeles. The Tibetan wool-and-silk rug was custom-made by Stark Carpet.

LEFT "In most residences, I like to design a dark, atmospheric room," said David of the study, which is located just off the living room. The burnished gold-tortoise wall covering from F. Schumacher & Co., the custom-made cowhide rug by Kyle Bunting at Holly Hunt, and the Osborne & Little grey chenille-covered sofa, with leather piping in the style of Jean-Michel Frank, lend the room its masculine look. The Bergamo wool draperies are the same color as the walls. In this room, the red accent is provided by the 1960s lacquered goatskin coffee table by Aldo Tura from Duane Antiques in New York. *Gypsy Red*, a 2011 painting by Tokyo-born artist Kikuo Saito, is a lively addition.

OPPOSITE The mix of textures includes a gilded-iron side table from Distant Origin, a shop in New York; the custom-made armchair of cognac-colored leather, trimmed in Makassar ebony; and a high-relief, ribbed cowhide rug.

PREVIOUS PAGES *Reds and Blacks, March 26, 2008*, a print by contemporary American artist Donald Sultan, offers a vibrant counterpoint to the neutral-hued dining room. The grass-cloth wall covering is by Phillip Jeffries. The 1970s sculptural floor lamp, with its three illuminated leaves, is by the Italian artist Tommaso Barbi, and came from Lobel Modern, in New York. The polished chrome starburst chandelier is from M.S.K. Illuminations, also in New York. The draperies were custom-made in a Calvin Klein silk from Kravet.

OPPOSITE David had the cherry wood dining table, which seats 14 people, custom-made in the style of the French Art Deco designer André Arbus. The black lacquer Art Deco-style chairs, from Artistic Frame, are upholstered in contrasting textiles: a leather and cream weave for the front, and a velvet for the back. Karim Ghidinelli, an Italian artist, created *Blue*, a 2011 etched aluminum with enamel work that has been hung between the windows.

ABOVE LEFT AND ABOVE The museum-quality French Art Deco sideboard, which was designed by Paul Follot in 1937, and came from Bernd Goeckler Antiques, was the clients' first major acquisition. It set the standard for many of the other pieces in the house. Included are a 1950s French Modernist round mirror, from Karl Kemp Antiques in New York, a pair of mirrored obelisks and a Murano glass vase from Lorin Marsh in New York. Along with the glass paperweights from Linda Horn, also in New York, the accessories contribute to the play on geometric forms in the room.

OVERLEAF Hand-blown Italian glass is one of David's favorite materials. The huge 12-light chandelier that hangs in the foyer is made of gold-dusted 1950s Murano glass. The 1940s Murano amethyst-colored chandelier, with its 12 scroll-like arms, is in the master bedroom. Both are Seguso fixtures that came from Newel in New York.

OPPOSITE To express both the clients' and the designer's shared love of Italy, David selected a fabric from Fortuny for the two-tone draperies in the master bedroom. The same pattern was continued as a stenciled frieze, painted by Dean Barger, along the wall. David designed the wood-and-leather custom-made headboard. The cut velvet is from Clarence House, as is the leopard print fabric on the long pillow. All of the linens were custom-made by Casa del Bianco in New York.

RIGHT Near the dressing room, a Biedermeier chest from Ritter Antik is the focus of an eclectic mix of accessories, including an Amaryllis lamp by Maison Charles, from Bernd Goeckler Antiques; a distressed gold-painted stool from Julian Chichester; and a Venetian mirror. The tufted ottoman, covered in aubergine mohair, was designed by David.

OPPOSITE The covered terrace at the back of the house has a view of a large rock that was on the property. The teak outdoor seating is all from Kingsley Bate. The teak-topped square table is from Holly Hunt; the polished concrete table was made by Bradley Hughes.

RIGHT A dining table from David Sutherland and chairs from Kingsley Bate furnish the dining area off the den.

A classically formal city residence is luxuriously brought up-to-date with textiles and furnishings of the highest quality

In putting together the elements for this impressive apartment, I paired velvet with silk, wool sateen with silver and bronze threads, and Ultrasuede with chocolate-brown embroidery. Geometric shapes, such as circles, squares, and rectangles, were used to offset those that were more organic. I enhanced the art with textiles, vintage and bespoke furnishings, lighting, rugs, and exquisitely crafted draperies. The home is cohesive as a whole, but each room maintains its own distinctive personality.

Although the decoration of this nearly 9,000-square-foot classical residence in Manhattan was completed in eight months, it was the culmination of an intense year with my clients. At the time, I was working with these long-term clients on building a contemporary house on Long Island. One of the goals was to include a lot of color, which the husband loves, even though his wife, who has a background in interior design and textiles, prefers neutral spaces. I began by removing the pediments on the doors, which were too formal, and reducing the size of some of the traditional moldings. I wanted to make the spacious rooms feel more appropriate to the twenty-first century. The choice of distressed French limestone in the foyer made the entrance more welcoming. Dark hardwood floors and textured rugs ground every room. While the apartment was still quite grand, it now had a "his"-and-"hers" quality. Ultimately, the renovation and decoration were all about creating a livable family space. I always strive to fulfill my clients' dreams in an imaginative way. They asked me to help them assemble a wonderful contemporary art collection of mostly American artists, and to make art an integral part of each room's design.

RIGHT To further emphasize the symmetry, David used pairs of rosewood consoles from Therien, keyhole-shaped mirrors in the style of French Art Deco designer Serge Roche that came from Jonathan Burden Antiques in New York, and 1950s Venini chandeliers from Lorin Marsh. The draperies, made of Bergamo wool sateen, have geometric embroidered edges by Penn & Fletcher.

OVERLEAF The 40-foot–long entrance gallery opens onto the living room and media room at one end, and the bedroom hallway and dining room at the other. Two vertical paintings by famous American artists—one, *Plaid*, a 1972 acrylic on canvas by color-field painter Kenneth Noland, bought from Sotheby's, and the other, a 1962 Morris Louis that came from the Riva Yares Gallery—fit perfectly, like sentinels between the doors.

PREVIOUS PAGES David selected furnishings to give the paneled room a tailored look. The sofa and armchair from Roman Thomas are upholstered in billiard cloth from Hines and a wool from Rogers & Goffigon; the bronze, brass, and glass coffee table in front of the sofa is from J. Robert Scott; the cream enameled-and-steel side tables are from Troscan at Holly Hunt. Between the two windows hangs *Untitled, 1972,* by Giorgio Cavallon, an Italian-born abstract painter.

ABOVE In the corner of the living room that overlooks Central Park, the walnut table and matching chairs are by the American designer William Haines. The set was specially made in 1959 for comedian George Burns' Hollywood house. The floor lamp is from Foscarini.

ABOVE The 1930s Italian Art Deco parchment table by Gustavo Pulitzer Finali came from Ed Hardy Antiques in San Francisco. The early 1960s ebony wood sculpture is by the French artist Alexandre Noll. The glass-and-chrome Italian lamp is a 1950s design by Fontana Arte.

ABOVE A 1950s high-back chair by American designer Tommi Parzinger, from Palumbo in New York, is paired with a 1930s French standing lamp and cigarette table from L'Art de Vivre, a gallery in New York.

ABOVE Draperies of Kravet flocked silk frame the view. A tripod floor lamp by David Weeks from Ralph Pucci in New York arches over a chaise by Roman Thomas, which has been upholstered in a Holly Hunt suede; the cast-bronze Bomarzo table by Eric Schmitt is also from Holly Hunt.

OPPOSITE AND RIGHT An arched doorway separates the living room, the apartment's former library, from the media room. Entirely paneled in a traditional warm golden pine, the room has been decorated to feel more contemporary. 1950s Murano glass lamps by Barovier & Toso have been placed on a chrome-and-glass console from Ralph Lauren Home. *Book of Clouds*, a 2007 work by Helen Frankenthaler, the American artist, hangs above the mantelpiece.

OVERLEAF The media room that faces Manhattan's Central Park was previously the living room of the apartment. David transformed it into a less formal, multi-functional space for the family to enjoy. *Pierre ou Paul*, a huge hand-hammered aluminum and platinum leaf light dome from Ingo Maurer, anchors the center of the room. Sofas and club chairs, upholstered in mohair or leather, by John Hutton for Holly Hunt, are both comfortable and contemporary. The custom-made shagreen coffee table with white bone trim was designed by Garrison Rousseau at Holly Hunt. The small glass and bronze side table is by Michele Oka Doner for Steuben. The painting on the far wall is *The Bird and The Cat*, a 1949 oil by Hans Hofmann, the German-born American Abstract Expressionist artist.

OPPOSITE AND RIGHT
Two 1980s paintings by
the Spanish-born Abstract
Expressionist artist
Esteban Vicente hang
above a pair of cast resin
consoles that were
designed by David and
made by Atta, a New York
company. At one end of
the room, *opposite,* a table
of cerused oak, parch-
ment, and inset leather is
meant for playing cards
or as an alternate dining
space. The husband loves
to play ping pong, so
David commissioned a
découpage mixed-media
regulation table, *right,*
from Tad Lauritzen
Wright, who is represent-
ed by the David Lusk
Gallery in Memphis.

OPPOSITE *Mysteries: Lumina Blue*, a 1999 painting by American artist Kenneth Noland, is centered over an early 1940s rosewood sideboard by Osvaldo Borsani that came from Bernd Goeckler Antiques in New York. The vivid blue 1950s Murano glass lamps came from Pierre Anthony Antiques in West Palm Beach, Florida.

RIGHT The reflection of a 1960s Venini Sputnik chandelier from Karl Kemp sparkles in an etched Italian mirror from Lorin Marsh.

OPPOSITE Dale Chihuly, the American glass sculptor, created the centerpieces on the dining tables. Each of the *Persian Sets* includes a series of different glass objects cradled in an irregularly shaped bowl.

ABOVE David designed the dining room to be completely original, bringing in the feeling of the outdoors with a bright green silk-and-wool twill carpet from Carini Lang that recalls the Great Lawn in Central Park. Two large square tables by Troscan are surrounded by a set of 16 chairs designed by Charles Hollis Jones in the 1970s. The large acrylic on canvas painting is *Delta Phi,* a 1960 work by American master Morris Louis.

OPPOSITE The wife's passion for textiles is evident in all the rooms, but especially in the sitting area of the master bedroom suite. A detail of the inlay of a 1905 rosewood Viennese desk by Karl Rajek, from Doris Leslie Blau in New York, coordinates with a flocked taffeta fabric from Rodolph.

RIGHT In a corner of the master bedroom, an armchair and ottoman from Dwellings Design are upholstered in a Bergamo wool sateen. The painting, *Alison Series: From the Window*, is a work by Esteban Vicente from 1976. The walls are upholstered in a Henry Calvin Ultrasuede.

OVERLEAF David designed the silk-mohair velvet-covered and ebonized mahogany bed, which is set between two alcoves in the luxurious master bedroom. The chaise and side tables are by Tommi Parzinger, from Palumbo; the American 1950s Modernist table lamps are from Karl Kemp in New York.

An extraordinary modern house with amazing views

and minimalist interiors makes an

elegant statement on the water

In this house I wanted the architecture and the furnishings to be integrated, so I made sure to use warm-colored materials and chose high-quality pieces with graceful lines to counterbalance the sharp angles of the building. The more organic additions to the design—the textiles, rugs, and accessories—inspired by sea glass, fossils, and driftwood, brought out the softer side of the minimalist interior. I chose outdoor fabrics throughout so my clients could come in from the beach and be able to sit on any chair. A group of artisans orchestrated the fine details.

Built from the ground up on a site on eastern Long Island, New York, and situated between the Atlantic Ocean and Shinnecock Bay, this house was a special and amazing project from the beginning. It was also a true collaboration between myself, the architect, and my clients. A family of four, they had been living in a contemporary beach house that was constantly in need of repair. They had thought about building a more traditional Shingle-style house, but after the time they had spent in the existing house, they decided they wanted a similar lifestyle—one that was open and that embraced the beach, the ocean, and the landscape. I knew that Alexander Gorlin, the New York-based architect, would be a good fit for this project. His approach to architecture as sculpture is in keeping with my aesthetic, and I felt my clients would agree. The upside-down house was the result of all of our talents and our combined vision. The beautiful vistas are just as much a part of the overall design as the minimalist details and functional interiors. Although the house has a certain grandness about it, it is neither fussy nor pretentious. My approach to the interiors was about achieving elegance through simplicity. The house, with its unifying staircase, is a piece of sculpture. The interior spaces flow seamlessly into one another, both vertically and horizontally. It has a life force that seems to be born from nature and the quality of being able to age beautifully, acquiring a gentle patina, and changing over time. This is a home that is forever!

PREVIOUS PAGES Seen from the dunes, the stone, glass, and wood house offers uninterrupted views of the ocean.

LEFT The front door, with its bronze hardware, cast from a piece of driftwood by New York artist Michele Oka Doner, opens onto the minimalist foyer. The screen, by Japanese artist Maio Motoko, is made from antique kimono fabric and sake bags, and entitled *Toki*, or *The Seasons*. The 1940s mahogany table is by Gío Ponti.

OPPOSITE The console, from Galerie Van den Akker, has been crafted from a solid piece of burled walnut. It is combined with an Hermès mirror from Karl Kemp, and an ammonite fossil, from Balsamo Antiques in New York.

RIGHT The main living space of the house is focused on the double-sided limestone and bronze fireplace. A floating staircase connects the different levels.

OVERLEAF A pair of limited-edition table lamps by French designer Hervé van der Straeten, from Ralph Pucci in New York, frame a wide view of the living room. The stoneware objects with a metallic glaze are by Pamela Sunday, an American artist. David always tries to place a side table within easy reach of the seating. The 1950s Edward Wormley table for Dunbar, with a travertine top, holds a collection of stoneware vases by American ceramicist Peter Voulkos, which were bought at auction.

LEFT Two sofas from Holly Hunt and the chair from Roman Thomas surround a bronze and glass coffee table, attributed to the 1970s Surrealist metalworker Philippe Hiquily, which came from Van den Akker Antiques. The *Cycladic Goddess* by the window is by Kevin Kelly and came from Guy Regal Ltd. in New York.

OPPOSITE The leather-covered swivel chair and ottoman are an Alfredo Haberli design from Moroso. The 1960s one-of-a-kind small sculptural table is by American designers Philip and Kelvin LaVerne, and came from Todd Merrill Antiques in New York. The pattern of the Carini Lang handmade silk living room rug was inspired by the ocean.

LEFT The dining area has been furnished with overscale white-leather–covered chairs from Holly Hunt and a 12-foot long table that has been cast in aluminum from a single slab of white oak by John Houshmand, a furniture maker in New York. Jacob Hashimoto, a New York- and Italy-based artist, created the 2009 *Slanting, the Sea, Silence,* an ethereal assemblage of Japanese paper discs that seems to float above the fireplace. The kite-like chandelier, called *Oh Mei Ma, Weiss* is by German designer Ingo Maurer.

OPPOSITE Opaque glass sliding panels allow the kitchen to be closed off from the dining room. A long grille, crafted in bronze by Michele Oka Doner, conceals the heating and ventilation systems. The mahogany, makore, and bronze credenza from Holly Hunt echoes the use of materials in the interiors.

OPPOSITE Dubbed the Sunset Room, the space that overlooks the bay is used for informal gatherings. A set of 1960s chairs by Osvaldo Borsani have been tucked into an oak game table.

RIGHT A sectional sofa from Moroso, upholstered in a terrycloth fabric from Lee Jofa, extends along one wall. The small pedestal tables have shagreen tops; the pillow is covered in an African Congolese tribal kuba cloth. The photograph, one of two, is by contemporary artist Renato Freitas.

PREVIOUS PAGES For the master bedroom, David designed a bed with a screen-like headboard that floats in the center of the room. The textiles include pillow fabrics from John Robshaw, as well as the embroidered duvet cover from Lee Jofa.

OPPOSITE David also designed the functional oval night tables of teak with a high-gloss marine finish; the fabric on the headboard, a synthetic from J. Robert Scott, is soft and practical. The sconce is by David Weeks.

RIGHT The 1950s French copper-tinted, mirrored credenza, with its bronze base and hardware from Karl Kemp, adds a feeling of glamour to the bedroom. David brought back the Venini vase from Venice as a housewarming gift.

LEFT The kitchen has an unimpeded view out to the ocean. The hanging lamps are from Nessen; the cabinets are from Boffi; and the table is an Eero Saarinen classic design for Knoll.

RIGHT A Duravit bathtub by Philippe Starck is freestanding in the master bathroom. The stool is a reproduction of a Pierre Chareau design from Urban Archaeology.

RIGHT The roof terrace, a perfect place from which to watch the sunset, was conceived to be like the upper deck of an ocean liner. Thousands of pieces of recycled glass create a water-like perimeter. Woven-mesh sofas by Tidelli from Walters Wicker have been used to sparsely furnish the space. The fireplace provides warmth on a cool evening.

A once-masculine Old-World apartment is softened and lightened to suit the needs of a new young family

I created a dramatic and eclectic interior by choosing furnishings that are textural and lush, with fluid and organic shapes. The color of the draperies matches that of the walls. Custom-designed silk rugs make a sophisticated statement and add to the warmth of the design. I treated the lighting, and especially the sconces, as pieces of sculpture—some bold and dramatic, others more delicate and intricate. They are all beautifully crafted and three-dimensional, like jewelry.

The apartment in one of the towers of the Eldorado—one of Manhattan's grand Art Deco buildings on Central Park West—was the third project I worked on for this client. In 2009, as relatively new parents of a baby boy, the couple wanted a larger residence that was to be elegant but also family friendly. It was time to pair the masculine style of the previous residence I had designed for the client in 2005 with softer, more feminine lines and colors, in an effort to combine both of their aesthetics. Using a few of the pieces from the client's previous apartment, I added new furnishings to impart a lighter and more contemporary feeling. The way the light came into the apartment, both during the day and the evening, was paramount—I wanted to make sure the spectacular 360-degree views were fully accessible.

LEFT The entrance foyer, with its silver-leafed ceiling, is focused on a large black and red painting by the American Abstract Expressionist Adolph Gottlieb, which gives the space a sense of drama. The Art Deco chandelier is from William Switzer; the 2009 *Dervish III* by Daniel Adel, a contemporary artist, hangs on the wall between the bedroom corridor and the dining room.

OPPOSITE The custom-made silk carpet, with its brushstroke pattern, was hand-woven by Carini Lang.

OPPOSITE The vignette on the Roman Thomas console in the foyer includes a Cubism-inspired nickel mirror, a pair of ceramic vases, a Colombian silver bowl, and a small abstract drawing on an easel, all from Flair Home.

RIGHT A mid-twentieth century Murano vase from High Style Deco, a shop in New York, has been paired with a kinetic sculpture by jewelry designer Robert Lee Morris from Skyscraper, a New York store.

OVERLEAF The large living room faces Central Park. A pair of Modernist 1940s slipper chairs from Galerie Van den Akker in New York has been upholstered in a Bergamo fabric with a metallic thread. An ebonized Flemish mirror, from Yale R. Burge in New York, makes a statement above the Art Deco-style mantelpiece that David designed. The print on the back wall is *Smoke Rings, Oct. 20, 2005,* by American artist Donald Sultan.

LEFT David likes to group pieces of furniture to create a play of shapes, contrasting colors, and different materials. In the living room, a gilded standing lamp, in the style of the French Art Deco designer Gilbert Poillerat, is juxtaposed with the black marble mantelpiece and elegant slipper chair.

RIGHT By the window, an Edward Wormley for Dunbar chair has been pulled up to a writing table by Madeline Stuart, the Los Angeles-based designer.

OVERLEAF A 1950s welded metal sculpture by the Italian-born American sculptor and furniture designer Harry Bertoia has been placed on the 1960s French bronze and glass Modernist table from Galerie Van den Akker.

LEFT In the living room, the painting by Latin American artist Raphael Soto, a classical stone torso, and a red lacquer cabinet create a lively composition.

RIGHT David wanted the library to be dark, enveloping, and full of atmosphere. The indigo glazed walls have been painted to look like faux-leather by Jennifer Hakker of Applied Aesthetics Painting Studio in Long Island, New York. David has worked with the artist since the beginning of his career. The custom-made sofa, from J&P Decorators, is in a wool flannel from Holland & Sherry. The lacquer and brass cocktail table, from John Boone, with its textured surface, subtly contrasts with the pattern of the wool and silk twill rug from Carini Lang. The photograph is by Elger Esser, a German photographer.

OVERLEAF Facing west, the dining room glows in the early evening. The Cedric dining chairs by John Hutton for Holly Hunt are covered in a waxed linen, also from Holly Hunt. A 1960s Murano glass chandelier is centered over the dining table. The painting is by William Quigley, an artist whose work the clients have collected over the years.

LEFT AND OPPOSITE
A warm ivory color was
chosen as the theme
for the dining room.
The sconce and credenza,
with its unusual brass
hardware, are both
re-issues of designs by
Tommi Parzinger from
Palumbo in New York.
The large 1970s faux-tusk
mirror is by Karl Springer
and came from Craig
Van Den Brulle, a shop
in New York.

OPPOSITE Her bathroom, with its mosaic marble floor, has been furnished with a black lacquer sink vanity that David designed. The walls, handpainted in a pattern of quince branches by Jennifer Hakker, lend an Asian feel to the room.

RIGHT Because it overlooks the reservoir in Central Park, David had the walls covered in de Gournay panels handpainted with Koi. Jonathan Browning designed the jewel-like sconces that frame the white enamel faux-twig mirror from Mecox Gardens.

A
Hamptons cottage
incorporates antiques with
lively objects
collected
over time in a charming
country
retreat

The first thing I did to my country house was paint the entire interior white. Then I used a sea-grass floor covering throughout to unify the rooms. Art has always been an inspiration and a jumping-off point for choosing a house's color scheme. As I had found an abstract Cubist still-life painting—a 'tongue-in-cheek' Picasso—I placed it over the fireplace in the living room, and used a red sofa as a punctuation mark and a unifying color. Blue silk taffeta draperies that evoke a wonderful ball gown dressed up the living room in an unexpected way.

I design emotionally, and never more so than in my own home. When I saw the perfect little Cape House with its "For Sale" sign in Water Mill, New York, I knew I just had to have it. When I stepped inside, however, the interiors were frightening: Each room was drastically different from another, and there was floral wallpaper everywhere. Yet I loved the way the shape of the house felt, and I could sense its potential. The house was the perfect setting for the furniture and possessions that I had been collecting for years from flea markets in England and France, and it felt wonderful to bring everything together in the same place. I mixed my classic, antique pieces with contemporary furnishings, which has always been my design aesthetic. As a Nantucket-style Cape House, it was the perfect space for combining various natural and warm woods. Like all of the master bedrooms I design, the one in this house, with its high ceilings and four-poster bed, is meant to be a restful sanctuary. The landscaping of the property and the exterior of the house are refreshingly uncluttered. An expanse of grass leads to the pond, and I surrounded the house with hydrangeas. A typical Cape with a sloping roof, the front door was the only exterior architectural element that would allow me to make a statement. My mother, who is an artist and from whom I inherited my natural sense of color, was instrumental in helping me pick its hydrangea blue color. It seems that every day, strangers drive into my driveway just to get a closer look at the front door.

PREVIOUS PAGES Two nicely weathered Adirondack chairs have been set up in the shade of the old oak trees in the back garden of David's country house in Water Mill, New York.

ABOVE Hydrangeas and boxwood topiary frame the entrance to the charming Cape Cod-style cottage.

OPPOSITE A British Colonial teak pillowed sofa sits in a corner of the wraparound screened-in porch. Ceramic garden stools act as low tables.

LEFT The living room, which spans the depth of the house, is the main gathering space. Ample seating includes a long sofa covered in a durable, tightly woven wool from Holly Hunt, with nineteenth-century French needlepoint pillows, and a pair of contemporary woven straw African stools. The pattern of the carpet, from The Rug Company, is of a stylized map of London.

OPPOSITE David often creates vignettes using some of the favorite objects that he has collected over time. A friend, the interior designer Mark Epstein, found the large, framed collage in a flea market in Paris. Treen, or wood-turned objects, a cast-iron inkwell, and a basalt urn are grouped on a late eighteenth-century English table that the designer bought at auction.

OPPOSITE Two antique French Directoire chairs, part of a set of eight, stand in front of the windows in the living room. The étagère is filled with David's collection of treen tobacco jars, vases, and small containers. The unlined blue taffeta draperies were made by Susan Gill in New York.

RIGHT A convex mirror, a 1911 charcoal drawing by American artist Francis Moylan Fitts, and a Thebes stool by Liberty are grouped in the living room near the foyer. The Biedermeier armoire was one of the first antiques that David acquired. A pair of colored engravings by Giovanni Battista Piranesi hang in the hall.

OPPOSITE In the dining area, a 1957 still life by Karel Lodewijk Bruckman, a Dutch-born artist who emigrated to Cape Cod, Massachusetts, hangs above a black lacquer Chinese credenza from Grey Gardens. David bought the silver-covered shells from Buccellati on a trip to Italy.

RIGHT The dining area is open to the screened-in porch, which allows it to be used for entertaining larger groups. The George III-style mahogany, satinwood, and tulipwood table was formerly in the collection of Albert Hadley, the famous interior designer, whom David greatly admires. The Anziano brentwood mahogany dining chairs from Donghia are a signature design in David's work because of their classical yet contemporary look. The Capiz shell chandelier is from Mecox Gardens.

LEFT The library is where David works when he is in the Hamptons. A French tailor's shop sign is above a sofa from John Saladino, a designer who has had an influence on David's work.

OPPOSITE The nineteenth century English desk is from Niall Smith in New York, and the antique Swedish chair is from Lorin Marsh. David's collection of rulers and tortoise-shell boxes date from his visits to the Portobello Road flea market in London.

J·PELTIER TAILLEUR

FAIT LES REPARATIONS

ROBERT KELLY

HOUSES OF THE HAMPTONS   GARY LAWRANCE
AND ANNE SURCHIN

OPPOSITE In the guest room, the ebonized-wood table that belonged to David's grandmother was carved to look like draped fabric. The antique wood tower is a pocket watch holder.

ABOVE The light-filled and spacious master bedroom is furnished with a four-poster bed from Oly Studio. A pair of French gilded overdoors have been put together to create a decorative quatrefoil. Black leather campaign chairs have been placed in front of a folding four-panel leather screen trimmed with nailheads.

NEW YORK CONTEMPORARY ART EVENING

Sotheby's

TUESDAY, MAY 15, 2007

A personal collection of Avant-Garde art

is paired with a sense of functionality in a light-filled city loft

My clients, who are both very visual, agreed with everything I was doing to make their space, located in New York's Chelsea neighborhood, function as a comfortable home. While one of them is extremely colorful and exuberant in personality and style, the other is a bit more restrained. I kept the architectural lines of the space and the shapes of the furniture in a contemporary vein, chose colors to make bold graphic statements, and used carpets to soften the overall feeling of the interior.

One of the greatest compliments is when good friends hire you to work with them on the design of their home. This was the case when a prominent art dealer and her partner, who is also well known and respected in the world of art and design, asked me to help them with their new loft space in Manhattan's Chelsea area. It was important that their home suit their ever-changing and impressive art collection, which ranged from oil paintings to sculpture to vintage furniture pieces. They asked me to make the most of their unusual art collection and to incorporate the different elements that each of them brought to the apartment. It was vital for me to integrate their styles and possessions and to create a cohesive environment that would feel like home to both of them. It was also imperative that I improve the interior structure of their new home. I first focused on creating a spatial flow in the loft. The high ceilings and light, which my clients absolutely loved, helped make the space look and feel much larger than it actually was. It was challenging to create a series of multi-functional spaces, but necessary to organize the existing elements in an architecturally pleasing way. The result is a comfortable loft with a quirky but stylish edge.

LEFT A large 2007-2008 mixed-media work by Los Angeles-based artist Mindy Shapero welcomes people in the foyer of the loft. Matthew Raw, a London–based artist, created *Moving Stories II*, a ceramic sculpture of a bag printed with news type.

OPPOSITE A graphic credenza by the Egyptian-born furniture and industrial designer, Karim Rashid, becomes the basis for a vignette that includes one of the clients' ancient Islamic and Phoenician iridescent glass pieces, an Art Nouveau Gallé lamp, and *Cut Flowers*, a 2008 print on metallic paper by Carter Mull, an artist who lives in Los Angeles.

RIGHT A sinuous sofa by Vladimir Kagan, the well-known furniture designer, anchors the main living area. It has been upholstered in a bouclé fabric from Glant; the throw pillow is from Dransfield & Ross. The vintage side chair and set of three occasional tables are from R.E. Steele Antiques, a shop in East Hampton, New York. The silk shag rug was custom-made by Carini Lang. The pewter pitcher, a 2007 work entitled *Hot Kettle en Aluminium et Chêne,* by Spanish designer Nacho Carbonell, is paired with *Untitled,* a 2010 wood piece by Gelitin, a group of four artists—Wolfgang Gartner, Ali Janka, Florian Reither, and Tobias Urban—who are based in Vienna, Austria.

ABOVE Pop artist Andy Warhol's
Interview 7 Volume Set stands at
the doorway to the sitting room.
The mid-twentieth century chairs,
upholstered in a fabric from Holly
Hunt, came from R.E. Steele Antiques.
Debris Pool, a 2003 painting
by Los Angeles-based artist Tomory
Dodge, has been hung above a
sectional sofa by Kagan.

OPPOSITE Paolo Buffa, a Milanese
architect, was the designer of the
late-1940s table, which came from Fred
Silberman, a New York antiques dealer.
Balloon Dog (Blue), a 2002 metallic
porcelain multiple by American artist
Jeff Koons, is on the table. The throw
pillows are from Dransfield & Ross. The
wool-and-silk rug is from Carini Lang.

LEFT *Frontal*, a 2010 sculpture of a chair with a broken back and seat by Jessica Jackson Hutchins, a Chicago-born contemporary artist, has been set up by the window in the sitting room. Andy Coolquitt, an artist who lives between Texas and New York, crafted the 2009 metal, wire, and light bulb piece called *Chair*, that leans against the wall.

OPPOSITE The mother-of-pearl and Lucite *C Table* is a 2010 piece by Nada Debs, a designer who lives and works in Beirut, Lebanon. The happy little figure is a Nana multiple by French artist Niki de Saint Phalle.

OPPOSITE AND RIGHT A
marble-topped table by
Finnish master Eero
Saarinen for Knoll is in
the dining area. The set
of faux-bois dining chairs,
which came from Lorin
Marsh, have been
upholstered in a striped
Paul Smith fabric from
Maharam. The Twiggy
floor lamp by Foscarini
stands in for a chandelier.

LEFT In the master bedroom, a vintage Egg chair and ottoman by Arne Jacobsen, the famous Danish furniture designer, was found at the Marché aux Puces in Paris, as was the mid-twentieth century floor lamp. *Untitled #4*, a collage by American artist Donald Baechler, is on the wall. The wool rug is by Carini Lang. The 2010 *Squid Table* is by Nada Debs; the porcelain vase is by architect Frank Gehry for Tiffany & Co.

OPPOSITE *Every Flower To You* is a 2005 ballpoint pen drawing on paper by American artist Jim Hodges, who also created the wallpaper in the powder room.

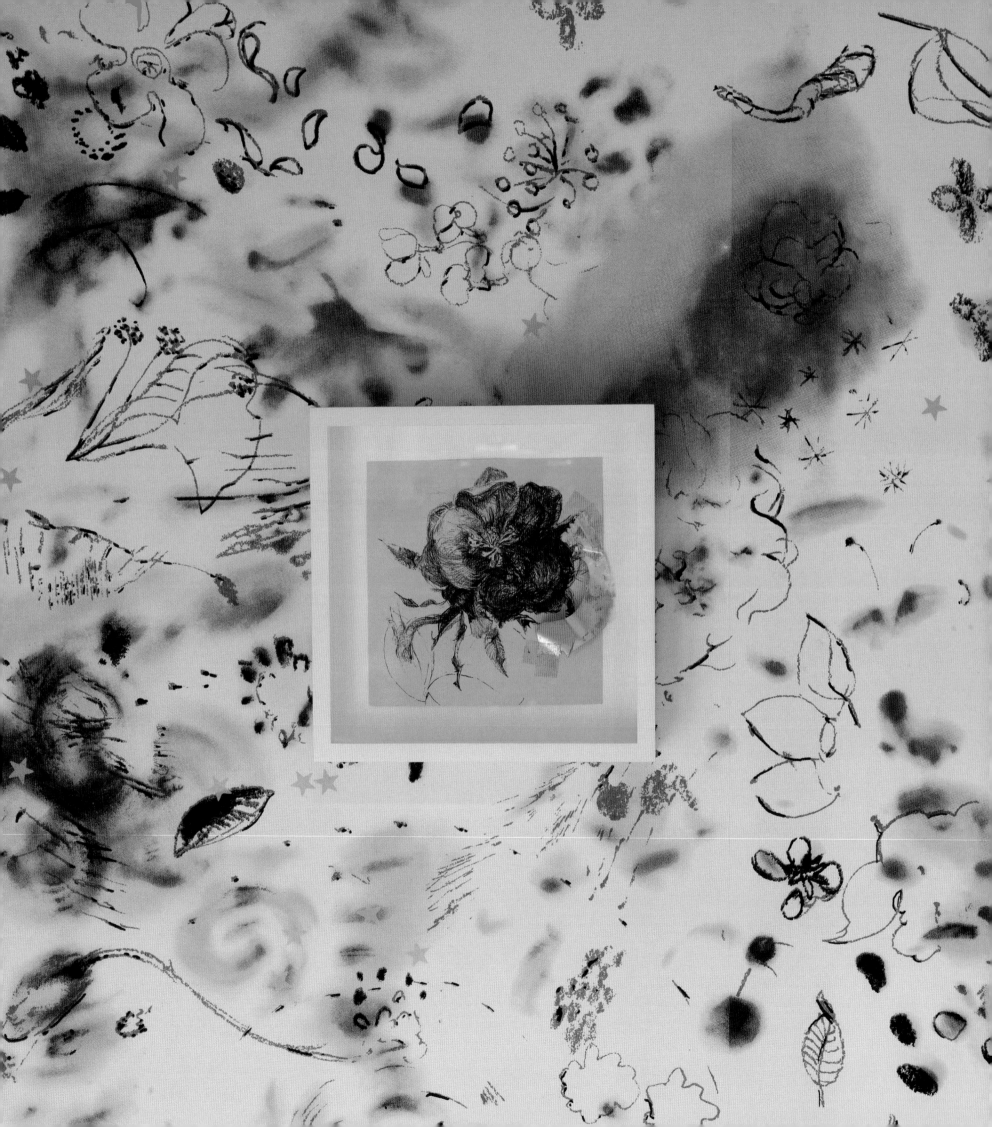

An estate in the desert that highlights great contemporary art and museum-quality antiques is both suitably grand and joyful

For this contemporary house out West, the clients were inspired by homes on the French Riviera, the Palladian villas of the Veneto, and classical buildings in New York and Palm Beach. The colorful palette of their collections took center stage. I chose warm golden tones for the backgrounds, from yellow to gold to caramel, to allow the art to breathe and to offset the antiques. The materials I chose were soft and sumptuous, using dozens of different luxurious fabrics—from chenille to wool sateen, ottoman cloth, and suede.

The owners of this extraordinary home, which took four years to complete, have been my clients since the beginning of my career. I have learned so much by working with them. Early on, we explored the auction houses and the best shops across the country and in Europe. This residence would be their main home, where they could accommodate their evolving collection of large-scale contemporary art. They had originally bought the desert property as a vacation home. Over time, they fell in love with the environment, purchased the adjacent properties, and we proceeded to create the estate they envisioned. The architecture was a collaboration between the homeowners, myself, and Vern Swaback, a local architect who had been a protégé of Frank Lloyd Wright. The clients' mandate was to design a contemporary villa with traditional elements that would fit in with the colors of the desert. Our relationship had grown over the years until I was considered a member of their family. I understood what they wanted, needed, and dreamed of—and made it a reality. With an architect on staff in New York, my office constructed all the interior drawings, and detailed the millwork. The interiors needed to be formal yet comfortable. It was a challenge to find just the right pieces of furniture, but my clients are perfectionists and, once they understood the scale, we were under way.

PREVIOUS PAGES At dusk, *Twins 1 & 2*, a 2009 work of painted stainless steel sculptures by Spanish artist Jaume Plensa, glows in the landscaped garden between the swimming pool and the house.

OPPOSITE AND RIGHT A contemporary interpretation of classical European villa gardens can be seen in the exterior spaces of the house, which include an arched colonnade and an outdoor sitting room and fireplace. The furniture was custom-made by McKinnon & Harris and upholstered in fabric from Chella. The seventeenth century majolica cistern is from Sotheby's.

RIGHT David Scott Interiors designed the grand double staircase with its balustrade of interlocking geometric iron and brass elements. Large-scale contemporary works of art, from the left, by Jean Dubuffet, Morris Louis, Fernando Botero, and John Chamberlain are dramatically set around the rotunda. The monumental William IV Padauk wood center table that dates from the mid-nineteenth century came from Florian Papp in New York. The late eighteenth-century neo-classical crystal chandelier was found at Therien, in Los Angeles.

OVERLEAF LEFT A nineteenth century neo-classical giltwood mirror, from Guy Regal in New York, which hangs over a rare eighteenth century Italian neo-classical console from C. Mariani Antiques in San Francisco, acts as an introduction to the formal elegance of the public spaces of the house.

OVERLEAF RIGHT In the hallway off the living room, a set of four 1986 works, entitled *Quatre Lithographies*, by the Dutch-born American Expressionist painter Willem de Kooning, have been hung near *White Women*, a trio of cast bronze figures by the American sculptor Manuel Neri.

PREVIOUS PAGES *Plowed Field*, a 1971 triptych by the American Abstract Expressionist Joan Mitchell, dominates the formal and elegantly furnished living room. Eighteenth century Italian Rococo giltwood armchairs, covered in a Cowtan & Tout silk damask, are arranged around a custom-made fruitwood and walnut cocktail table from Lorin Marsh. The sofa is upholstered in fabric from Lee Jofa.

OPPOSITE *Maquette for Stairs*, an early 1990s bronze piece by British sculptor Lynn Chadwick, is a contemporary counterpoint in the living room. The hammered gold vase is by Pomellato.

RIGHT A 1974 stabile by American sculptor Alexander Calder entitled *Crag with White Flower and White Discs* provides a strong graphic statement in the traditionally furnished living room. The English Regency ottoman, one of a pair, is upholstered in a Jim Thompson silk.

OVERLEAF Two paintings—one early, one late—by the American master Hans Hofmann, the 1940 *Still Life with Fruit and Coffee Pot*, on the left, and the 1965 *Proprie Moto* on the right, flank the fireplace in the living room. The antique Italian Rococo mirror was bought at auction from Sotheby's. The obelisks on the mantelpiece, and the spheres on the Carole Gratale glass and gilded bronze tables, are part of their large collection of rock crystal objects.

PREVIOUS PAGES *Empire Blue Chandelier,* a 2000 sculpture by the American glass artist Dale Chihuly, is the focus of the Water Room, a circular space off the living room that offers a cool and relaxing respite from the desert heat. Pop artist Roy Lichtenstein's 1994 *Brushstroke Head,* an enamel on nickel-plated bronze sculpture, Dubuffet's 1973 *L'Accueillant,* and a number of papier mâché nanas by French sculptor Niki de Saint Phalle provide strong notes of color in the monochromatically furnished room. The club chairs from A. Rudin are covered in fabric from Holly Hunt; the custom-made curved reed sofas from the American Wing are in a fabric from Zimmer & Rohde. The rug, with its wave-like pattern, was custom-made by Stark.

OPPOSITE In the breakfast room, sixteenth-century majolica pieces, bought at auction, are paired with the china place settings in the Siesta pattern from Hermès.

RIGHT The circular room links the interior of the house to the surrounding landscape. A chandelier by Karl Springer is above a dining table from Kneedler-Fauchère that is surrounded by Art Deco-style chairs from J. Robert Scott.

LEFT An impressive collection of ceramics by Pablo Picasso fill the shelves in the family room. A large glass-topped coffee table from Lorin Marsh fills the center of the room and is convenient for storing and displaying oversize art books.

OPPOSITE Chilean-born, twentieth-century artist Roberto Matta's 1985 *Reservoir du Temps (Mine of Time)*, stretches along one wall. A bird-shaped Picasso ceramic vase stands on a Louis XVI-style guéridon from John Boone.

OPPOSITE In the master bedroom suite, a watercolor by French Pointillist Georges Seurat hangs above a nineteenth century Viennese Biedermeier ebonized chest from Ritter Antik in New York. The Donghia chair came from the clients' former home. The mid-1930s French alabaster urn-shaped lamp, one of a pair, is from Bernd Goeckler Antiques in New York.

RIGHT The bed, with its mirrored posts, is from Nancy Corzine, and has a headboard upholstered in a sateen from J. Robert Scott. The Susan Gill Work-room in New York made the bed curtains using a Donghia fabric. The swing-arm gilded bronze sconce is from Christopher Norman. The custom-made bed linens are from Casa del Bianco.

OPPOSITE AND RIGHT
The dining room was
conceived as a romantic
place in which to enter-
tain in the evening. David
designed the antiqued
mirror panels that reflect a
nineteenth century
English chandelier, from
Nesle in New York. The
George III sideboard
dates from the eighteenth
century. The English
Regency arm and side
chairs, from Lorin Marsh,
covered in a Zimmer &
Rohde fabric, surround a
Regency mahogany
dining table from antiques
dealer Florian Papp.

ABOVE *Still Life with Sculpture*, a 1974 painting by Lichtenstein, seems to glow above the sofa in the paneled library.

ABOVE AND OPPOSITE English eighteenth- and nineteenth-century architectural models of staircases, part of a large collection of small-scaled examples of fine craftsmanship, are displayed on the coffee table. A particularly spectacular example of a double stair is in one of the galleries, *opposite*.

OVERLEAF LEFT The clients have a passion for movies and often entertain friends at private screenings. The well-appointed theater lobby is furnished with a sofa and club chairs, all from Phoenix Custom Furniture, which are covered in fabrics from Robert Allen and Glant. The coffee table is by Karl Springer; the 1930s table lamps are from Karl Kemp & Associates in New York; and the pair of striking George III satinwood and tulipwood cutlery urns were bought at a Christie's auction.

OVERLEAF RIGHT The custom-designed screening room is the work of Theo Kalomirakis, who is known for his opulent installations. The starry-sky–like fiber optic ceiling is by lighting designer Walter Spitz.

An apartment on Miami Beach for family and friends, with wonderful open spaces, captures the colors of the ocean

The interiors are intended to capture the feeling of the beach, which can be seen from the floor-to-ceiling windows—with colors that come from the sand and sea. The idea was to create a low-maintenance, ready-to-wear environment. Everything is about the ease of living in Florida—an urbane and cool style with a slight edge. I was inspired by the first photograph we purchased—an image by contemporary artists Mike and Doug Starn, of *Big Bambú*, the extraordinary sculpture they installed on the roof of the Metropolitan Museum of Art in New York.

These long-term clients, whose homes I had previously done in Southampton, New York, and Manhattan, were thrilled to have me decorate their new winter getaway home in Miami Beach, Florida. This home for a family of four was to be an escape destination where they and their friends could go and immediately relax. The 3,600-square-foot residence that combines three apartments would have all the amenities and services of luxury hotel living. The public spaces flow into each other without any boundaries. The neutral palette of the walls brings into focus the unique contemporary art collection. The breathtaking views catch your eye the moment you enter. Weathered teak is utilized for the cabinetry, reinforcing the earthiness of the design. Unique pieces come from regional sources, as well as from visiting such fairs as Design Miami and Art Basel Miami. Many of the chairs were chosen for their sculptural look. There is a sensuality in all the furnishings I select. I think about how one line relates to the next, and am always creating harmonious, subtle relationships between all of the pieces. Because this home is for relaxing as well as entertaining, the furnishings are all extremely comfortable and low maintenance, yet possess a certain sophistication. Even the flooring throughout, an epoxy polished concrete, has a durable yet earthy quality. I created an environment where textures, furnishings, and accessories are layered seamlessly, and in which my clients can enjoy their own version of Miami Beach.

RIGHT The main living room opens onto a panoramic view of Miami Beach, the bay, and downtown Miami. It has been furnished with a custom-made four-seat sofa from Lost City Arts, New York, which has been upholstered in one of Perennials' outdoor fabrics. The architectural floor lamps are from Mitchell Gold + Bob Williams. The wooden coffee table, from Miami shop Jalan Jalan, has been made out of cut branches and resembles driftwood, contributing to the beach-like feeling of the apartment.

OPPOSITE On the wall that divides the main living room from the lounge hang two 1960s French artworks, one concave and one convex, which both came from Objectiques, a shop in New York. They evoke the weathered wood used throughout the apartment.

RIGHT A limited edition photograph of a detail of *Big Bambú*, the monumental construction created by American artists Mike and Doug Starn, anchors the living room. Lounge chairs from Ralph Lauren Home, upholstered in a white fabric from Mokum, recall Miami Beach's Art Deco origins.

OVERLEAF David created a comfortable enclosed niche for a daybed to act as a transitional space between the lounge and the main living room.

OPPOSITE AND RIGHT In the living room, a 1970s Optical Disk sculpture, with inspirational poetry by American artist Mary Bauermeister, is centered on a custom-made credenza. The tufted slipper chair, one of a pair in the room, is upholstered in a fabric from Holly Hunt.

OVERLEAF LEFT Italian architect and furniture designer Gabriella Crespi crafted the unusual cork, bark, and silver box that reinforces the naturalistic feeling that David wanted for the space. David found it at Vermillion, a shop in Miami. It sits on an ottoman that has been upholstered in a fabric from Pindler and Pindler in an abstracted African pattern.

OVERLEAF RIGHT Egg-shaped silver-leaf low tables from Mecox Gardens have been set on a custom-made wool-and-silk area rug from Edward Fields.

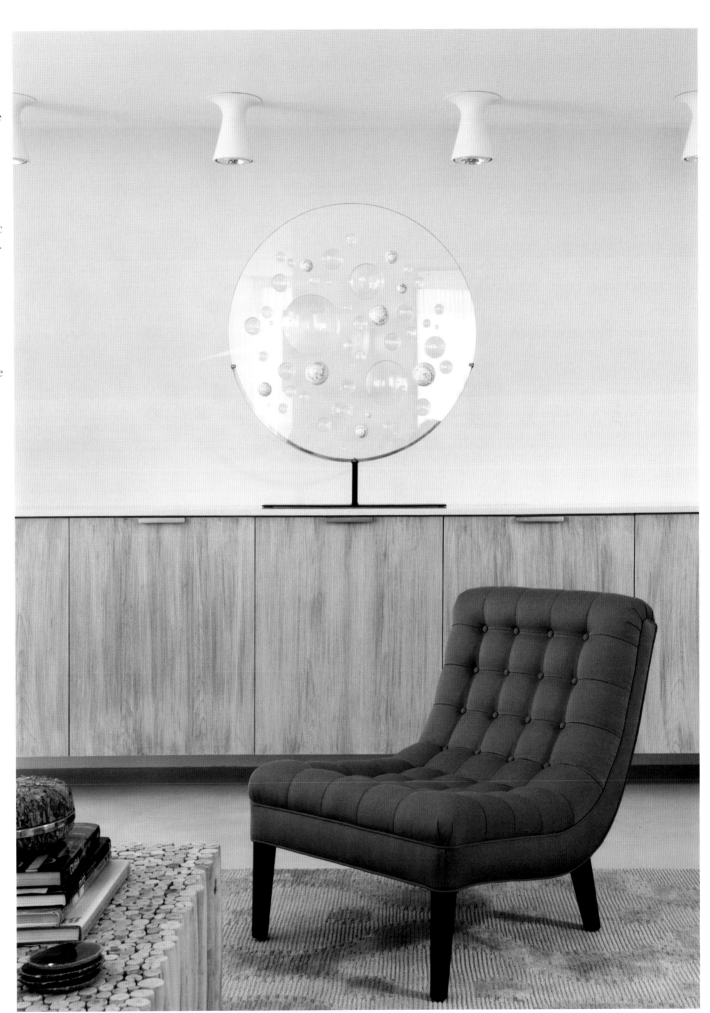

LEFT The white metal wall-mounted console for D & A Labs, with its dozens of small cut-metal walking figures, is by Isolde Pringiers, an interior designer from Belgium. David discovered the piece at Design Miami. The concrete light sculpture that incorporates watch parts is a French 1975 design from Gallery 440 in New York.

RIGHT *Blush*, a 1978 print by American artist Kenneth Noland, which came from the Estate of New York restaurateur Elaine Kaufman, hangs above a 1950s sideboard by American designer Paul McCobb in the dining room.

LEFT AND RIGHT David designed the master bedroom in tones of white, ivory, and celadon. The furnishings were selected for their organic modern shapes. Included are a cast resin mirror from Oly Studio, a pair of free-standing fiberglass room dividers by Don Harvey from Thomas Hayes in Los Angeles, and the inlaid bone night table from Homenature in Southampton, New York. The Egg Chair and ottoman are by Danish furniture designer Arne Jacobsen.

ABOVE The seating area in the master bedroom overlooks the ocean. The chaise is from Lost City Arts, the pillows are from Calvin Klein Home, and the silver-coated reclaimed Douglas fir table and the lamp by Verner Panton are from Design Within Reach.

ABOVE A pair of Jens Risom chairs and an ottoman, all from Ralph Pucci, New York, provide a comfortable reading area at one end of the dining room.

ABOVE AND ABOVE RIGHT Off the dining room and kitchen, a terrace has been furnished with a pair of Mu daybeds from Dedon, which have been upholstered in fabric from Donghia. The ceramic square side table is from Comerford Home in Bridgehampton, New York. The centerpiece, set on the dining table from Crate & Barrel, is a cast resin bowl filled with glass globes. It came from Ankasa, a shop in New York.

An English-style country manor set on open fields takes on a striking and contemporary graphic look

The rich brown coloration and earth tones used throughout the rooms were derived from the dark chestnut floors, the beams in the double-height living room, and the stone hearth. The English waddle wall treatment in the living room, a technique that combines hay with plaster, evokes the feeling of a barn. This interior is all about textures and natural materials—sisal, crewel, and linen. I punctuated the neutral tones with gold, green, and burgundy. It is a house that unfolds, and I wanted to continue the sense of layering on the interior.

I first started working with this client, a bachelor with two teenage daughters, in 2004 when I helped him find and then decorate his Manhattan apartment, a co-op in the San Remo—an historic Art Deco building on Central Park West. I understood his needs and his personal style, which helped when I went with him a year later to look for a country retreat on the south shore of Long Island, New York. Even though we had already established a rapport from our previous work together, I still did the same professional presentation that I do with all of my clients. In this case, I knew he wanted a year-round escape in the Hamptons that wasn't a typical Shingle Style Colonial home with whitewashed, casual interiors. His mandate for the project was also for a residence that didn't require much construction. He purchased the house in March, giving me barely three months to accomplish everything in time for him to enjoy the summer season. The only structural modification I made was enclosing the porch, which added additional living and dining areas. The English Cotswold-style house had a good structure and the architectural feeling that he was looking for. Designed by New York-based architect Alan Wanzenberg, with interiors by Arthur Dunham of Jed Johnson Associates, Inc., it had the added benefit of being on a knoll with an expansive lawn that stretched down to a pool and guesthouse. The 6,000-square-foot house is situated next to large open fields, giving the bachelor and his family complete privacy. Great care had been put into the original house, and all it really needed was great furniture and a range of textures to give it character, including unique rugs in variations of geometric patterns, from squares to rectangles to linear designs, to give the rooms a subtle added dimension. The house ended up evolving into an expanded home with the arrival of a baby boy for my client and his lovely new partner.

LEFT AND OPPOSITE Architect Alan Wanzenberg built the Shingle Style house in Bridgehampton, New York, to look as if it had always been there. David particularly likes the entrance, as it is partly hidden behind sculpted boxwood and climbing hydrangea.

PREVIOUS PAGES David added the screened-in porch to extend the entertaining areas of the house. The rattan sofa and chair and the custom-made concrete and iron coffee table are from Mecox Gardens. The ottomans and deck chair are from David Sutherland. All of the outdoor fabrics are from DeLany & Long, in Greenwich, Connecticut.

OPPOSITE The French vintage oiled leather chair in the high-ceilinged living room came from Lorin Marsh and, with the Chinese root stool from Mecox Gardens, adds to the masculine feeling of the room. The bronze standing lamp came from Objet Insolite; the Chinese black-lacquered étagère is from Evergreen Antiques in New York; the antique rosewood wheel on the top shelf is from Tucker Robbins in New York; and the folk-art fish was found at Privet Cove, a shop in Southampton, New York.

ABOVE LEFT AND ABOVE The living room has the feeling of a sophisticated converted barn. The iron chandeliers belonged to the previous owner and David felt they were perfect for the space. The designer created two seating areas with sofas in a Jean-Michel Frank style, made by Phoenix Custom Furniture, which have been covered in a Rogers & Goffigon linen. The cowhide ottomans came from Mecox Gardens. The bronze and glass tables are from Lorin Marsh; the sisal area rug is from Stark Carpet.

ABOVE AND ABOVE RIGHT The dining room is set in an octagonal turret that lends itself to being furnished with a large round Italian table, from Mecox Gardens. The comfortable overscale high-backed chairs are also from Mecox Gardens. The crewel leaf-patterned fabric of the draperies from Lee Jofa has a strong graphic look. The sconces and chandelier are from Roman Thomas.

OPPOSITE The walls in the entrance foyer—and throughout the main core of the house—have been painted by Jennifer Hakker of Applied Aesthetics Painting Studio in Long Island, New York. The antique Swedish chest of alderwood root is from Evergreen Antiques; the faux-twig mirror and the lamp are from Lorin Marsh.

OVERLEAF The wide upstairs landing that overlooks the entrance foyer and living room has been enlivened with a play of graphic elements, including Hakker's wall treatment, and a striped cotton dhurrie from Stark Carpet, which references the two-toned balustrade and railing.

OPPOSITE, RIGHT, AND BELOW RIGHT David chose handmade graphic rugs and dhurries to give the interior a more contemporary feeling while reflecting the arts and crafts look of the house. On the landing, *opposite*, he chose a patchwork carpet that has been made of a series of natural-colored textiles; in one of the guestrooms, *right*, the rug is a striped cotton dhurrie; and in the master bedroom, *below right*, another patchwork in reds, blues, and yellows acts as a foil to the neutral palette of the room. All of the rugs are from Stark Carpet.

A superb site on the ocean and unique furniture for adventurous clients

Situated at the end of a long private road and set on the Atlantic Ocean, the glass and limestone house, *overleaf,* was designed by the New York-based firm 1100 Architect. The clients are forward thinking, so we chose unique pieces of furniture, such as a copper-and-glass cabinet by Patrick Naggar and the Cloud table by Guy de Rougemont, which both light up from the inside, and one of French artist Yves Klein's coffee tables, with its extraordinary blue pigment. I wanted the outdoors and indoors to flow into each other, so I chose a neutral background, and fabrics with strong textures—linens, cottons, and outdoor fabrics—in beige and taupe. I specified the use of brushed stainless steel hardware throughout. The house will culminate in a green roof planted with sea grasses—the architects' bold concept—to make it look as if it were rising up from the surrounding landscape.

index

PHOTOGRAPH CREDITS

Architecture by 1100 Architect Rendering by VIZE, 224-225

Antoine Bootz, Front cover, 1-9, 14-15, 16-30, 32-33, 35, 36-61, 62-85, 86-87, 91, 94-105, 110-111, 130-138, 141, 143, 144, 146-159, 160-189, 190-207, 208-209, 210, 214, 216, 217, 218-219, 220 Back cover

© Ron Chapple | Dreamstime.com, 12

CLM/Shutterstock.com, 13

© Czalewski | Dreamstime.com, 13

© Fancy Collection/SuperStock, 12

Marili Forastieri, 11, 31, 34, 112-129, 139, 140, 142, 145

Ruslan Kokarev/Shutterstock.com, 12; littleny/Shutterstock.com, 13

© MIVA Stock/SuperStock, 12

Michael Moran: 88-89, 90, 92-93, 106-109

Ron Niebrugge/Wild Images, 12; Chris Pole/Shutterstock.com, 13

© Peter Van Rhijn/SuperStock, 13

George Ross Photographs: 211, 212-213, 215, 216, 221

stavklem/Shutterstock.com, 13

Virunja/Shutterstock.com, 12

Krivosheev Vitaly/Shutterstock.com, 12

acknowledgments

I dedicate this book to my wonderful family and friends, and to the memory of my dear friend, Lorraine Schacht. Their encouragement and love has been unwavering and I am deeply grateful.

My thanks, first of all, to all of my clients and their families who for twenty years have invited me into their lives, put their faith in me, and allowed me to create their dream homes. Their support and trust have made it possible for me to fully develop my talent. I particularly want to acknowledge those who have granted me permission to feature their homes in this book. It has been an incredible experience to work with all of them: Holly Andersen and Doug Hirsch, Judy and Andy Ban, Carl Barbato, Laura and George Bilicic, Renee and Stanley Blau, Jill Braufman and Daniel Nir, Mark Brennan, Siobhan Carty and Phil Marber, Carla Chammas and Judi Roaman, Iris Chernok, Deborah and Alan Cohen, Adam Derrick and Robin Steakley, Victoria Elsberg, Helene Fagin and Sid Silberman, Jill and Mark Fishman, Sir Roland and Lady Nina Franklin, Atilano Gimenez and Arnie Guior, Dorothy and Peter Gold, Ron and Alzbeta Harvey, Joy and Gil Helman, Nisha and Brian Hurst, Jean and Ron Jacobs, the James Hotel Group, Megyn Kelly and Doug Brunt, Steven Lavietes, Sally and Howard Lepow, Ronni Mann and David Brodsky, Jill and Doug Meyer, Harriet and Bernard Miller, Linda and Herb Morey, Stacey Moritz and David Brodsky, Aideen and Joel Mounty, Lyn and Roy Neff, Janice and Scott Pierce, Joan Pompadour, Corrine and Bob Raicht, Rick Reddy, Jonathan Ressler, Ellise and Eric Rose, Morleen and Jack Rouse, Jorge Saeta and Alonso Salguero, Eddie Schwartz and Russell Vance, Carolee Shubert, Ludmilla and Marc Siegel, Beatrice and Jeff Stein, Kathleen Sullivan, Robynn, Robert, Andrew and Scott Sussman, Fran and Mike Tancer, Karen and Mark Taub, Jennifer and Derek Trulson, Larry Van Valkenburgh, Sophie Wade and Gerry Cardinale, Bunny and Jim Weinberg, Nancy Weiner, Judy Witt, and George Zuber.

My success would not have been possible without the dedication and hard work of my incredible staff. Some are still with me, others have moved on, but all have contributed greatly. I am especially grateful to my design director, Douglas Roach, my "right hand," for his tireless efforts, talent, and wonderful sense of humor. Thanks also to Lucio Amadio, Pauline Ba, Toka Ball, Jason Beckwith, Claudia Blandford, Charles Burleigh, Ron Czjaka, Alan Gilmer, Wade Hui, Heidi Korsavong, Kimberly Latham, Elly Poston, Kelly Quinn, Michael Reiman, Kate Scheuring-Quinn, Maggie de la Vega, and Nancy Wanek. A very special thanks to my nephew and former business director, Matthew Pober.

Our projects have been enriched by so many talented craftsmen, designers, and artisans. I am proud to have had the privilege of working with Fred Agrusa, Leo Avlonitis, Michael Bagley, Dean Barger, Lupe and Fabrizio Biasiolo, Ed Bulgin and the entire crew at Bulgin Associates, Joe Carini, Jack Clarke, the entire DiSalvo family, Elizabeth Dow, Howard Elkowitz, Edwina von Gal, Susan Gill, Gary Gordon, John Gregoras, Gary Greenwald, Perry Guillot, Jennifer Hakker, John Hite, Hamilton Hoge, Dennis Hopper, John Houshmand, Jeff Lupien, and everyone at Kitchell Custom Homes, Ron Krieb, Chris LaGuardia, Joseph and Suzanne Landa, Juan Londono, Pino Licul, James Mansfield, Lee Markbreit, Elliot Mazzocca, Sophie Mallebranche, Nathan Orsman, Penn & Fletcher, Gary Seff, Walter Spitz, Brian Stair, Christy Ten Eyck, Dan Thorp, Louis Tori, Jim Tribe, Walid Wahab, Gary Waleko and the Men at Work crew, Bud Webb, Sue Wellot, Walter and Jonathan Wirth, and Jodi Xuereb.

I am continually inspired and grateful to all the architects we've collaborated with on our many projects: Scott Ageloff, John Baldessari, Paul Benowitz, Reid Betz, Rick Cole, James Davis, Randy Falk, Harry Fishman, Alexander Gorlin, Sebastian Kaempf, Anthony Pellino,

David Piscuskas, Mark Proicou, Meredith Colon-Reiman, Juergen Rheim, Will Schulz, Dipti Shah, Carl Shenton, Vern Swaback, and Mike Wetzel. Over the years, so many wonderful art and antique dealers have been supportive and encouraging. Among them are Doris Leslie Blau, Dallas Boesendahl, Lee Calichio, David Duncan, James Elkind, Bernd Goeckler, Fred Imberman and Robert Israel, Karl Kemp and Gilberto Oliveros, Miles McEnery, Todd Merrill, Alice, Mindy and William Papp, Guy Regal, Meg Wendy, and Dennis Yares.

Building this book, like our projects, has been an extensive process and has required a collective effort of so many talented people. I would like to thank:

Suzanne Slesin, my friend and publisher for her incredible enthusiasm and encouragement. She and her talented team at Pointed Leaf Press—Nyasha Gutsa, Regan Toews, Deanna Kawitzky, Marion D.S. Dreyfus, and Rebekah Fasel—carefully managed all of the moving parts so deftly.

Stafford Cliff for his design genius: He distilled and captured my style, and with Dominick Santise Jr., gave the book its shape.

Antoine Bootz for the magical photographs that grace these pages, as well as the stunning images captured by my dear and talented friend, Marili Forastieri. Thanks also to Michael Moran and George Ross for their beautiful photographs.

Barbara Dixon for her thoughtful, in-depth interviews.

I am so grateful to Michele Oka Doner for writing the Preface. She is a true inspiration, friend, and collaborator.

A very special thank you to Mark Rose for contributing his incredible talent by creating the most beautiful floral arrangements, but most of all for his friendship.

I am greatly appreciative of the New York School of Interior Design (NYSID), where I found the artist inside me and where I learned to think outside the box. The many dedicated teachers and the entire board have been tremendously supportive over these many years. I am so proud to still be a part of this incredible institution. I would also like to thank the editors and writers who have featured my work in their publications. Among them are Sian Ballen, Sallie Bradie, Paulina Canalas, Doris Chevron, Kendall Cronstrom, Julie Dannenberg, Sarah Firshein, Lesley Hauge, Rebecca Ho, Jason Kontos, Bobbie Leigh, Paige Rense, Anne Sanchez-Osorio, Jenny Sherman, Judith Thurman, Loren Landoc, and Samantha Yanks.

I am grateful for my family and friends, who have cared for me and nurtured me: the Pober family, and especially my beautiful sister, Cindy; the Rotfeld family, and most of all my incredible aunt Karen and uncle Dolph; and my wonderful mother, Judy. My friends, Stefano Antoniazzi, Keith Bacon, Brandon Bass,

Carl Barbato and John McCroan, Dean Beaudreau, Marty Berger, Noel and Liz Berk, Jose Castro and Nathan Orsman, Michael DeMeo, Brian Doyle, Jamie Drake, Mark Epstein, Helene Fagin, Brad Frey and Justin Scalzo, Lenny Fried, Joie Gamboa, Carmen Goyette, Allison and Zachary Julius, Patrick LaVacca, the Ledy Family, Peter Lentz, Mimi Levitas and Sarah Wilsterman, Peter Lentz, Louis Marra, Gregory Marshall, Manolo Medina, Marnie McBryde, Alex Pashkowsky, Jason Penney, Elizabeth Pienczykowska, Alonso Salguero, Tom Samet and Nathan Wold, Caryn Schacht, Lorraine Schacht and Sherry Mandell, Marge Schneider, Tito Romagnolo de Laurentis, and Gary Zimberg. A very special thank you to Ron Talarico, whose love and support have been unequaled.

David Scott—November 2011/June 2014

David Scott Interiors
www.davidscottinteriors.com

FRONT COVER A 2008 photograph entitled *Bronzino: Ugolino Martelli*, by the German artist Reinhard Görner, sets the scene in the atmospheric library of David Scott's apartment in New York.

BACK COVER *Plowed Field*, a 1971 triptych by the American Abstract Expressionist Joan Mitchell, dominates the formal and elegantly furnished living room in a house designed by David Scott.

OPPOSITE TITLE PAGE David Scott was photographed on location in the West of the United States, in front of a painting by the American artist Joan Mitchell.

ABOVE LEFT Josie, *left*, and Ethan, David's long-haired dachsunds, are at home in his Water Mill house.

OPPOSITE A high-relief, ribbed cowhide rug adds texture to a Connecticut interior.

Michele Oka Doner is an internationally acclaimed artist whose prolific career spans four decades. Her work—encompassing sculpture, public art, drawings, prints, functional objects, artist books and video—is fueled by a lifelong study and appreciation of the natural world from which she derives her formal vocabulary. Her work is represented in numerous prominent art museums and private collections in the United States, Europe, and the Middle East, including the Metropolitan Museum of Art and the Whitney Museum of American Art in New York, the Art Institute of Chicago, and Le Musée Des Arts Décoratifs, at the Louvre, in Paris.

Pointed Leaf Press is pleased to offer special discounts for our publications. Please contact info@pointedleafpress.com for details or visit our website at www.pointedleafpress.com.
Printed and bound in China.
First edition/second printing
10 9 8 7 6 5 4 3 2
Library of Congress Control Number: 2011944795
ISBN 13: 9780983388951